The Library of the Five Senses & the Sixth Sense™

Sight

Sue Hurwitz

The Rosen Publishing Group's
PowerKids Press™
New York

Published in 1997 by The Rosen Publishing Group, Inc.
29 East 21st Street, New York, NY 10010

First Edition

Book Design: Kim Sonsky

Photo Credits: Cover and all photo illustrations by Seth Dinnerman.

Hurwitz, Sue, 1934–
   Sight / by Sue Hurwitz.
     p.   cm. — (Library of the five senses & the sixth sense)
   Includes index.
   Summary: Explains the sense of sight, including how the eye works.
   ISBN 0-8239-5055-7
   1. Vision—Juvenile literature. [1. Vision. 2. Senses and sensation. 3. Eye.] I. Title. II. Series: Hurwitz, Sue, 1934– Library of the five senses (& the sixth sense)
QP475.7.H87 1997
612.8'4—dc21
                                         96–29958
                                            CIP
                                            AC

Manufactured in the United States of America

CONTENTS

1   Carlos   4

2   What Is Sight?   6

3   How Do You See?   8

4   Your Eyes   10

5   Parts of Your Eyes   12

6   Your Lens and Your Retina   14

7   Sight and Your Retina   16

8   Sight and Your Brain   18

9   Eyeglasses   20

10 Having Healthy Eyes   22

    Glossary   23

    Index   24

Carlos

Carlos goes camping with his family during the summer. He likes to look for different kinds of birds, trees, and flowers. Sometimes he watches raindrops fall onto leaves. Carlos always looks for rainbows after a rainstorm.

One day Carlos watched a long line of ants during the family picnic. The ants marched toward the picnic blanket. Carlos ran and picked up his food. He didn't want to share his lunch with those ants!

What Is Sight?

Sight is one of your **senses** (SEN-sez). Your senses tell you what is happening to you. They also tell you about the world around you. Your eyes work like a camera. When your eyes are open they take pictures of what you are looking at.

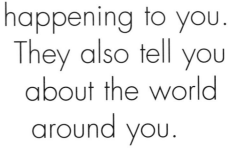

6

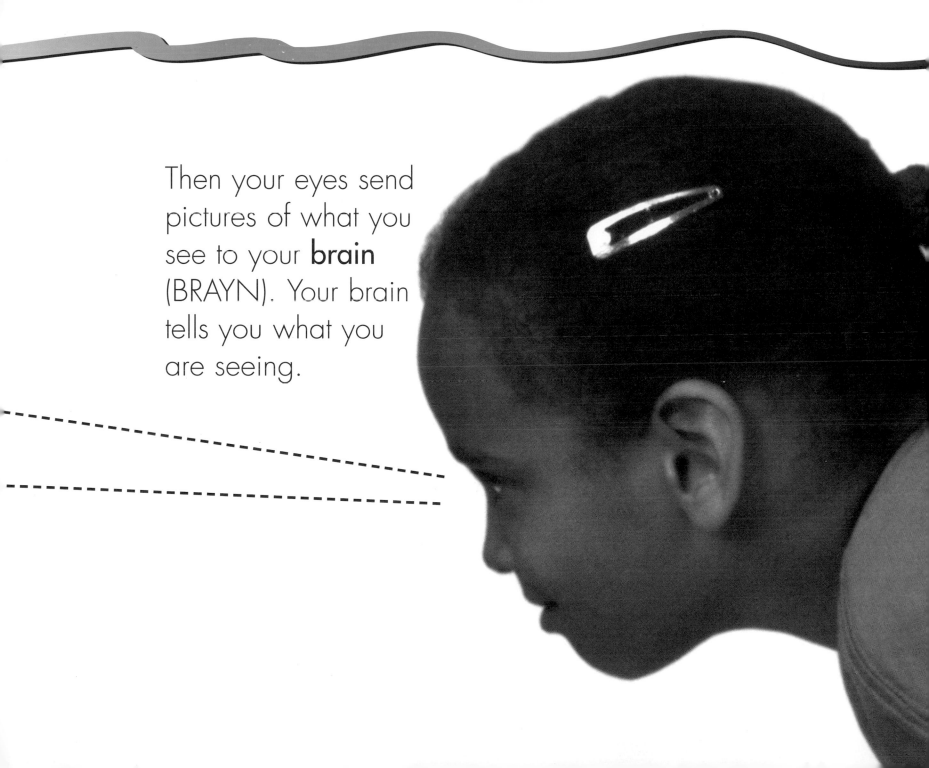

Then your eyes send pictures of what you see to your **brain** (BRAYN). Your brain tells you what you are seeing.

How Do You See?

You already know that you see with your eyes. But how do your eyes work? Light **rays** (RAYZ) bounce off the things that you look at. The light rays travel in a straight line to your eyes where they form pictures. Your brain stores the pictures that your eyes send to it. Of course, you cannot see in the dark or

8

when your eyes are closed!

Each eye has six muscles to move it. Your eyes can move up, down, right, or left. Some animals have eyes that work separately. But both of your eyes work together.

Your Eyes

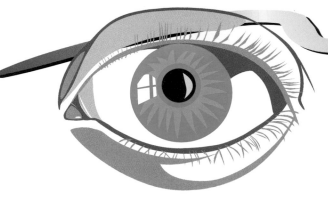

Eyes are shaped like balls.
They are filled with a clear, jelly-like liquid. Most of the
eyeball is inside your head. Light enters the eye through

BLUE EYE

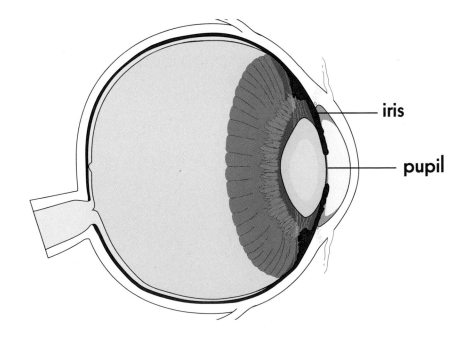

iris

pupil

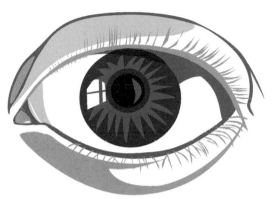

the **pupil**
(PYOO-pul). The
pupil is a small,
dark hole in the
middle of a large colored circle.

The colored circle is called the **iris** (EYE-ris). Most irises are blue, brown, green, or hazel. Your irises may be the same color as one of your parents' irises.

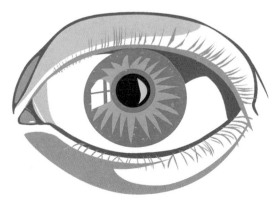

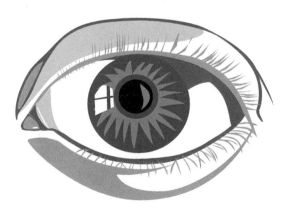

11

Parts of Your Eyes

The iris is a **muscle** (MUSS-ul) that changes the size of your pupil. Pupils get smaller when bright light hits them. The pupil protects your eye from too much light. The pupil gets larger in low light. The larger pupil lets more light into your eyes to help you see better.

The **cornea** (KOR-nee-uh) is a clear covering that protects the outside of the iris and pupil from dust and germs. The cornea is like a curved window. It bends light rays to form pictures as light enters the eye.

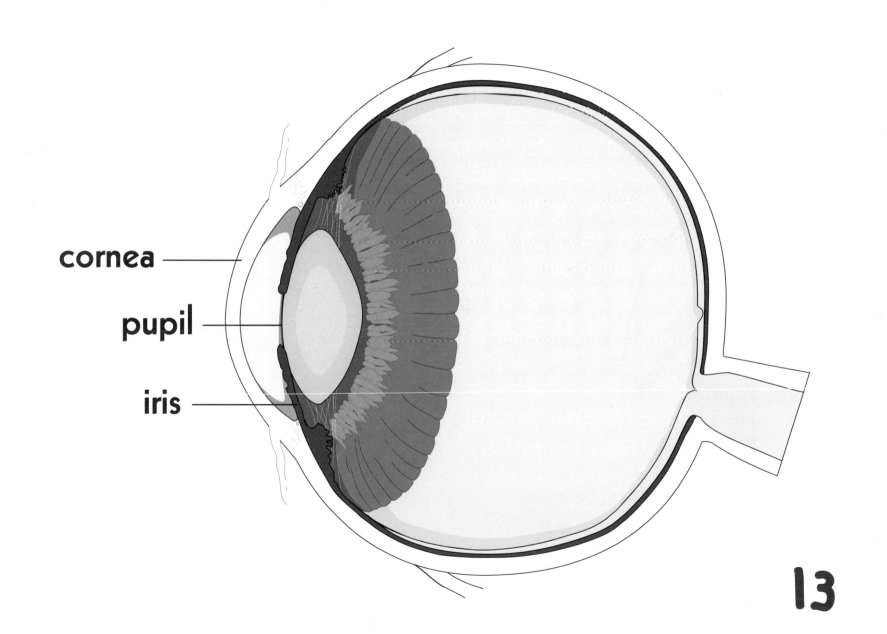

cornea

pupil

iris

13

Your Lens and Your Retina

Light travels through the pupil to the **lens** (LENZ), which is behind the iris. The lens is hard, curved, and clear. It directs the way you see light. What you see is turned upside down and backwards by the lens and is flashed onto the **retina** (RET-in-uh).

The retina is like a screen at the back of the eye. It has millions of tiny

14

nerve cells (NERV SELZ). The nerves carry messages about what you see to your brain.

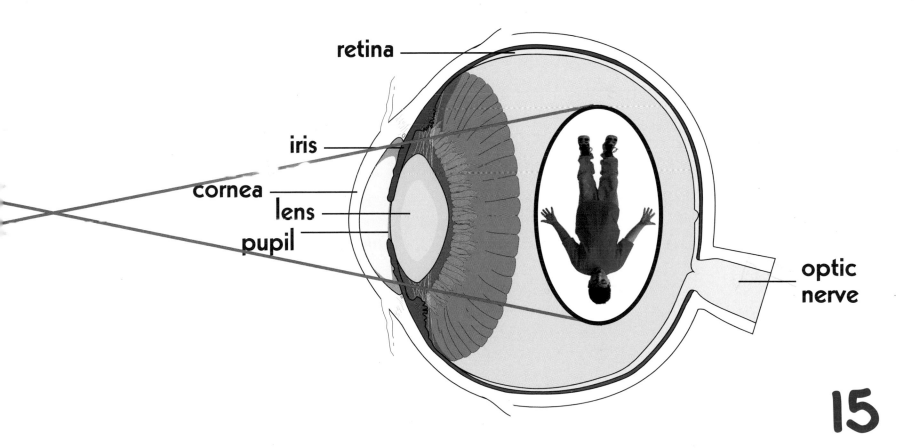

retina

iris

cornea

lens

pupil

optic nerve

15

Sight and Your Retina

The retina has two kinds of cells. They are called rods and cones. The retina has about 125 million rods. Rods are skinny cells around the sides of the retina. They tell you about different **shades** (SHAYDZ) of gray. Rods help you see at night.

The retina has about 6 million cones. Cone cells are fat and scattered around the retina. Cones allow you to see colors. Cones also let you see in bright light.

It's important to keep your rods and cones healthy. They need lots of vitamin A. You can get vitamin A from foods such as carrots.

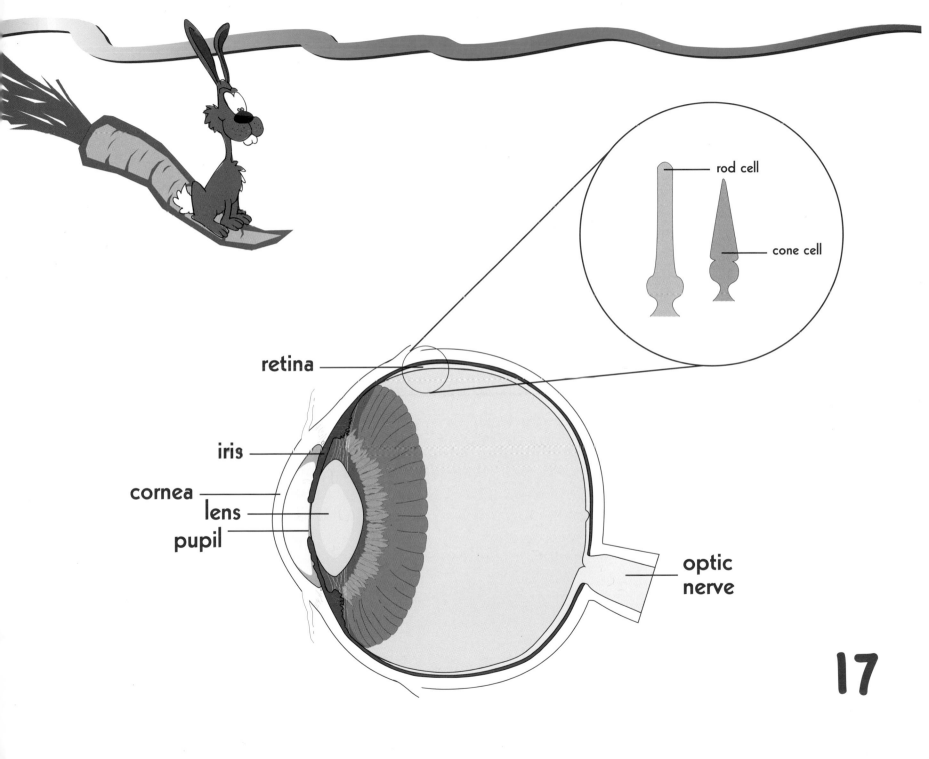

rod cell

cone cell

retina

iris

cornea

lens

pupil

optic
nerve

17

Sight and Your Brain

Messages about what you see are carried to your brain through the **optic nerve** (OP-tik NERV). The optic nerve carries pictures, or images, to the brain from the retina.

But the images on your retina are upside down and backwards! Your brain must put the images back the right way. Then it can make sense out of what you see.

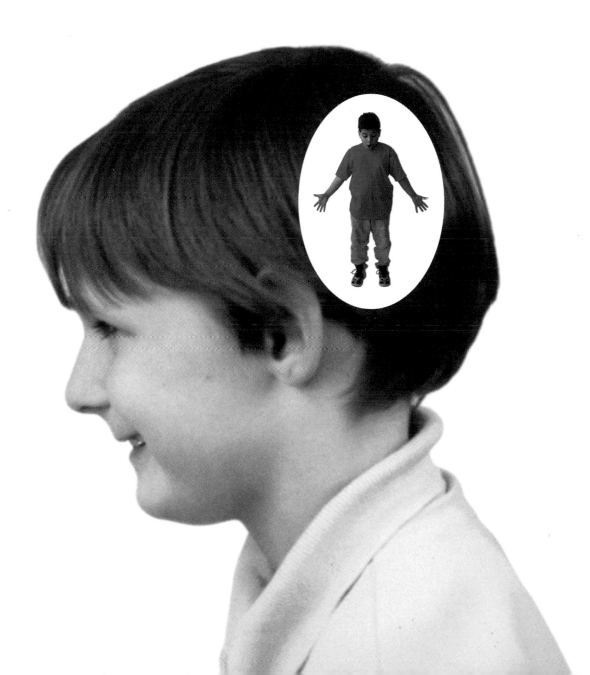

Eyeglasses

You may have sight that is not quite perfect. Images on your retinas may not be formed very well. If you only see things clearly when they are near you, you're **nearsighted** (NEER-sy-ted). If you only see things clearly when they are far away from you, you're **farsighted** (FAR-sy-ted).

Doctors can fix these problems with eyeglasses. If you get headaches or have to squint to see clearly, you may also need eyeglasses. About half of the people in the United States wear eyeglasses.

Having Healthy Eyes

There are some important things to remember about keeping your eyes healthy.

👓 Never look directly into the sun. That can hurt your eyes.

👓 If your eye itches, try not to rub it—whatever is making your eye itch could scratch your eyeball.

👓 Keep sharp or pointed things away from your eyes. You could damage the cornea or scratch your eyeball.

👓 Read only in bright light. Reading in poor light could strain your eyes.

👓 Have your eyes checked once a year by a doctor. Take care of your eyes and they should last you a lifetime!

Glossary

brain (BRAYN) The main nerve center in your head. The brain controls everything that your body does.

cornea (KOR-nee-uh) The clear covering over the iris and pupil.

farsighted (FAR-sy-ted) Seeing distant things more clearly than near ones.

iris (EYE-ris) The colored part of the eye that surrounds the pupil.

lens (LENZ) The clear part behind the pupil and iris that sends pictures to your retina.

muscle (MUSS-ul) Part of the body that is used for movement. You have muscles all over your body.

nearsighted (NEER-sy-ted) Seeing things that are near more clearly than things that are far away.

nerve cell (NERV SEL) The building blocks of nerves, which send messages to your brain.

optic nerve (OP-tik NERV) A bundle of nerves that carries pictures, or images, to your brain.

pupil (PYOO-pul) The dark opening in the middle of the iris that lets light enter the eye.

ray (RAY) A line of light that comes from a bright object.

retina (RET-in-uh) The lining of the eye that acts like a screen. The cornea and lens send light onto the retina.

senses (SEN-sez) The ways your body learns what is happening to you and the world around you.

shade (SHAYD) A slight difference from the original.

23

Index

B
brain, 7, 8, 15, 18

C
cells, 16
cones, 16
cornea, 12, 22

E
eye, 6–7, 8–9, 10, 12, 22
eyeball, 10, 22
eyeglasses, 20

F
farsighted, 20

I
iris, 11, 12, 14

L
lens, 14
light, 8, 10, 12, 14, 16, 22

M
muscle, 12

N
nearsighted, 20
nerve cells, 15

O
optic nerve, 18

P
pupil, 11, 12, 14

R
rays, 8, 12
retina, 14, 16, 20
rods, 16

S
senses, 6
shades, 16
sight, 6, 20